REEL TIME

PUBLISHED BY CREATIVE EDUCATION AND CREATIVE PAPERBACKS
P.O. BOX 227, MANKATO, MINNESOTA 56002
CREATIVE EDUCATION AND CREATIVE PAPERBACKS
ARE IMPRINTS OF THE CREATIVE COMPANY
WWW.THECREATIVECOMPANY.US

DESIGN AND PRODUCTION BY CHRISTINE VANDERBEEK
ART DIRECTION BY RITA MARSHALL
PRINTED IN THE UNITED STATES OF AMERICA

PHOTOGRAPHS BY ALAMY (CI2), CORBIS (BOB ROWAN/PROGRESSIVE IMAGE),
DREAMSTIME (SPENCER BERGER, MICHAEL GRAY, ALEKSANDER KOVALTCHUK,
LISAMARIE, DANNY SMYTHE), ISTOCKPHOTO (ANDY_BOWLIN, EASY_
ASA, MARTIN MCCARTHY, MOLOKO88), SHUTTERSTOCK (PITCHAYARAT
CHOOTAI, COPRID, ALEKSANDAR DICKOV, DIGOARPI, GRAFVISION, IOFOTO,
KOKHANCHIKOV, KRASOWIT, DUDAREV MIKHAIL, SERGEY NIVENS, RONTECH3000,
STEVENRUSSELLSMITHPHOTOS, TAVIPHOTO, DAN THORNBERG, JEFF THROWER,
VECTORPIC, WWW.BILLIONPHOTOS.COM, MANSILIYA YURY)

LIBRARY OF CONGRESS CATALOGING-IN-PUBLICATION DATA
ROSEN, MICHAEL J.
GONE FISHING / MICHAEL J. ROSEN.
P. CM. – (REEL TIME)
INCLUDES INDEX.
SUMMARY: A PRIMER ON THE BASIC DOS AND DON'TS OF FISHING, INCLUDING TIPS
ON THE BEST TIMES TO GO FISHING, ADVICE ON HOW TO PREPARE FOR A FISHING
OUTING, AND INSTRUCTIONS FOR MAKING A BUG LURE.

ISBN 978-1-60818-772-0 (HARDCOVER)
ISBN 978-1-62832-380-1 (PBK)
ISBN 978-1-56660-814-5 (EBOOK)
THIS TITLE HAS BEEN SUBMITTED FOR CIP PROCESSING UNDER LCCN 2016010299.

CCSS: RI.3.1, 2, 3, 4, 5, 7, 8, 10; RI.4.1, 2, 3, 4, 7, 10; RI.5.1, 2, 4, 10;
RF.3.3, 4; RF.4.3, 4; RF.5.3, 4

FIRST EDITION HC 9 8 7 6 5 4 3 2 1
FIRST EDITION PBK 9 8 7 6 5 4 3 2 1

GONE FISHING

→ MICHAEL J. ROSEN ←

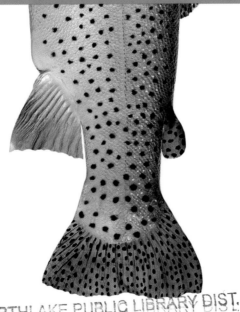

CREATIVE EDUCATION ⚓ CREATIVE PAPERBACKS

GONE FISHING → CHAPTER 1

TIME FOR FISHING

As you peek out the window early in the morning, it's still dark, but the sky is clear. It is going to be a perfect day for fishing! The best times to fish are in spring and early fall. The water temperature is just right then. Too early or too late in the year, the weather will be cool. The fish will be sluggish and slow to strike. Try to get to the water in the early morning or early evening. That's when fish usually feed.

Check the weather forecast. Typically, a nice day means good fishing. When it's not too hot or cold, too cloudy or windy, too hazy or humid, conditions are just right.

fishing rod

drinking water

tackle box

lunch or snack

bait

polarized sunglasses

For a successful trip, you'll need more than a stocked **tackle** box, handline or rod, and bait. Think about when and where you will be fishing. What else might you need? Plan ahead. Make a checklist, so you don't forget anything!

hat

life jacket

FISHING CHECKLIST

- [ ] sunscreen of at least SPF 30

- [ ] a hat or visor

- [ ] insect repellent

- [ ] long pants and socks
  To protect against thorns and poison ivy.

- [ ] shoes you won't mind getting wet or muddy
  Make sure they have good traction if you'll be on a slippery dock, boat, or rocks.

- [ ] lunch or a snack
  Bring a cooler, too, if you need to keep food cold.

- [ ] drinking water

- [ ] a **creel** or cooler
  If you plan to take home your catch.

- [ ] a minnow net
  If you need to catch minnows for bait.

- [ ] a minnow bucket
  To hold your bait.

- [ ] cloth gloves
  For handling and releasing fish.

- [ ] a first-aid kit

- [ ] a life jacket
  If you'll be on a boat or near deep water. Or if you are still learning to swim!

- [ ] polarized sunglasses

- [ ] a landing net

- [ ] a camera or sketchbook
  For a quick "capturing" of your fish.

- [ ] a tape measure
  To measure your catch.

- [ ] a radio
  With earbuds or headphones.

- [ ] a poncho or raincoat
  If there is a chance of rain.

- [ ] a pocket knife
  Be sure to have an adult's permission!

FINDING FISH

Carp like to hide in cloudy waters and will nibble at most kinds of bait.

N ow that you have everything you'll need, it's time to fish! But where do fish gather in a body of water? The likeliest places are called prime lies. Prime lies provide fish with four key things: They offer shelter from predators, sources of food, plenty of oxygen, and a place to rest in faster currents.

For example, a boulder in a stream softens the current's flow. It also offers protection. The current carries food right past the fish. So instead of tossing your line just any old place in the water, think like a fish. Look for the things they need.

A fish that's hiding in a prime lie will be facing into the current. Walk upstream as you look for a prime lie. You will be able to sneak up, unnoticed, behind the resting fish. Quietly cast your line out in front of the prime lie. While the fish has its guard down, you can deliver your bait right to it!

*Even with a perfectly cast line,
fish may ignore your lure and bait.*

GONE FISHING → CHAPTER 3

ANGLING ADVICE

Just like the fish you aim to catch, lures come in many different shapes, sizes, and colors.

When fishing near other anglers, look at the tackle they're using. Ask questions. Anglers spend lots of quiet time patiently waiting for fish. But that doesn't mean they don't enjoy talking. Most jump at the chance to give advice to young anglers.

At a tackle shop, you might ask a salesperson or even another customer: "Do you know of a nearby spot for bass?" or "What have the trout been biting on lately?"

But keep in mind that each angler deserves to fish without too many interruptions. The first person to arrive at a body of water should be

Don't fight over the fish!

respected by later anglers. New arrivals should fish downstream. That way, they won't catch fish the others may have met upstream. At a pond, choose a spot far enough away so that your line will not cross another's. And always speak softly, so you do not bother people—or the fish!

Some fish, such as salmon (pictured), swim in groups called schools.

NOT A NIBBLE?

Trout strike quickly, which can make them more challenging to catch.

You may have wonderful equipment, a fully stocked tackle box, the perfect fishing spot, and the right bait—but not a single nibble! Perhaps the fish just aren't biting where you are today. What can you do? Move on. Try again later. Or, simply enjoy the time away from technology and busy streets. Savor all that the natural world has to offer on this particular day.

Anglers constantly wonder *how* and *why* and *what if*. The lure that was lucky yesterday might be a dud today. The fish that were here last week may have moved on. Finding, attracting, and hooking fish is a puzzle that anglers try to solve with each and every cast.

So that "invisible tackle box" you always bring along may need a few extra sections. One for mysteries, another for unanswered questions, and a third for good guesses. Add a secret compartment of determination … just to keep from giving up. And don't forget a giant spool of luck! Sometimes, it's just plain luck that counts when you toss your hook into the water.

Try casting your line wherever there is water!

ACTIVITY: BUG LURES

A LURE CAN BE USED OVER AND OVER TO ATTRACT FISH. MAKE YOUR OWN "BUG" LURE WITH BITS AND PIECES OF RECYCLED MATERIALS.

MATERIALS

- scissors
- a small piece of sponge
- rubber bands
- an inch-long feather
- a nail
- waterproof glue
- a #4 or #6 hook

1 Add a drop of glue to the hook's shaft. Push it into the sponge. The eye of the hook should poke out of the sponge. Some of the shaft and the bend of the hook should be sticking out the other side.

2 Using a small nail, poke a little hole in the back of the sponge. Poke another small hole above the hook's bend, and two on the sponge's side.

3 Put a dot of glue on your small feather. Stick it into the hole above the hook's bend.

4 Cut strips from your rubber bands. Put a dot of glue in the three other holes. Push the rubber band strips into each one.

5 Allow the lure to dry completely. Then tie it to your line and try your luck!